THE HERMITAGE

SLAVIA
ART BOOKS

General Editor Dr. Mikhail Piotrovsky

Introduced by Liudmila Torshina

Edited by Olga Fedoseyenko
and Irina Stukalina,
with the assistance of Anna Barkhatova

Translated from the Russian by Alexandra Georges

Photographs by Vladimir Terebenin,
Leonard Kheifets, Victor Savik

Main Lay-out by Olga Fedoseyenko
Lay-out and computer-aided makeup by
the Megas Design-Bureau, St. Petersburg

ISBN 5-88654-046-6

THE HERMITAGE

The Hermitage is a celebrated museum, the pride of Russia and her northern capital, St. Petersburg. The Hermitage houses more than three and a half million monuments of art and culture. These include paintings, sculptures, drawings and engravings, the richest collection of works of the applied arts and more than one million coins and medals and archaeological and cultural artefacts. In the Hermitage the entire history of culture and art of the peoples of Europe and the East from the most ancient times until the twentieth century appear before the visitor. The Hermitage occupies five buildings in the centre of St. Petersburg being one of the most beautiful architectural ensembles. It includes the Winter Palace, the former residence of the Russian emperors, the Hermitage Theatre and also the museum buildings proper—the Small, Old and New Hermitages. The exhibition dedicated to the early eighteenth-century history of Russian culture is displayed in the Menshikov Palace on Vasilyevsky Island.

The Hermitage. View of the museum from the Neva

The museum was initiated in 1764 when Empress Catherine II owned the Berlin merchant Johann Ernest Gotzkowski's collection of 225 paintings. She made it her goal to establish her own palace gallery which would possess collections no less famous than those of European monarchs. On her instruction, through the intermediaries of the best art connoisseurs of the time, both entire collections, as well as individual works of art, were purchased at European auctions; and commissions were made from prominent artists. The Empress gave herself up with pas-sion to the collection of gemstones. By her own admission she suffered from the "gemstone sickness". Towards the close of Catherine II's reign the Hermitage collection numbered 3,000 paintings, almost 7,000 drawings and more than 70,000 engravings, as well as 10,000 carved stones and 38,000 books. Already at that time the Hermitage was considered to possess one of the richest palatial collections in Europe. In the subsequent era following Catherine the Great's reign, additions to the Hermitage became more and more systematized: the museum acquired

monuments of art which were needed to provide a comprehensive reflection of the history of art.

Thus in the 1830s–1860s antique relics were actively purchased in Europe; the largest acquisition of the Empress at that time was the Marquis of Campana's famous collection. In the 1830s archaeological research began in southern Russia and the Hermitage was enriched with the most valuable works of ancient Greek and Scythian art. From a private palatial museum such as it was under Catherine II, the Hermitage by the mid-nineteenth century had already been transformed into the most outstanding European museum of world art.

The immense palace of the Russian emperors, built in the eighteenth-century Baroque style, is a majestic and elegant edifice. Its southern façade with wide patterned cast-iron gates, with mighty columns spanning two stories and with sculptures over the cornice, faces Dvortsovaya (Palace) Square. The northern façade with its high porch stretched along the Neva, with its rhythm of snow-white columns echoing the coursing of the river's waves, as it were.

Nothern façade of the Winter Palace

Unknown artist
of the second half of the 18th century
Portrait of Catherine II
in a Travelling Dress

The western and eastern façades with their rezalites are turned towards the city: the eastern part is hidden behind the Small Hermitage adhering to it, while the western façade, concealing a small, charming garden, looks through the wide street onto the ancient Admiralty building. At this site, at the time of the erection of St. Petersburg in the early eighteenth century, palaces, the residences of dignitaries, as well as of the founder of the city, Emperor Peter I, stood. Empress Anna Ioannovna settled in one of them in the early of the 1730s. After her, her successors also lived here during the winters. Russian power grew and expanded; the might of Russian monarchs intensified and in 1754–62 at the site of the decayed old "Winter Residence", the chief architect of the Russian court, Francesco Bartholomeo Rastrelli, erected the new Winter Palace corresponding to the dignity and brilliance of the Russian autocracy.

The Winter Palace. View from Palace Square

The 1917 revolution transformed the Imperial Hermitage into the State Hermitage. During the course of almost 80 years of the twentieth century the museum collections expanded almost fourfold. In the first years following the revolution the Hermitage received the most lavish private art collections, nationalized by the Soviet government. In the 1930s–1940s a series of Leningrad and Moscow museums were closed by the government; their collections, for example, French paintings of the nineteenth—twen-

tieth centuries, found refuge in the Hermitage. A constant source of additions to the Hermitage were scientific, archaeological and collecting expeditions. Thus were amassed the collections of Scythian art and of ancient Altai art, old Russian icons, monuments of art from Central Asia, China and Tibet. Works of art, acquired through the Hermitage Purchasing Commission, at international auctions and presented by collectors and contemporary artists, merged with the Hermitage collection.

Luigi Premazzi. 1814–1891
View of the New Hermitage from Millionnaya Street
1861. Watercolour

Portico of the New Hermitage

Side by side with the departments already established as far back as the eighteenth and nineteenth centuries—the Departments of Western European Art, the Ancient World and Numismatics — in 1920 and 1931 the Oriental Department and Department of Archaeology were founded respectively, which were followed by the Department of the History of Russian Culture in 1941.

The Hermitage did not remain aside from the terrible ordeals which befell Russia's lot in the twentieth century. At the end of the 1920s — early 1930s the museum lost a part of its treasures. According to the shortsighted decree of the government they were sold to foreign buyers. More than fifty works of art, Raphael's *Madonna Alba*, Titian's *Venus with a Mirror*, Rubens' portraits of Isabella Brant and Elena Fourman (the renowned *Fur Coat*), Rembrandt's *Portrait of Titus*, Watteau's *Mezzetin* and a series of others, are now in the museums of Europe and the United States.

11

Winter Canal

Northern façade of the Winter Palace

The Rastrelli Gallery in the Winter Palace

During the years of the Second World War the Hermitage experienced all the tribulations of Leningrad's 900-day blockade. As early as the commencement of the Great Patriotic War (1941–1945) the museum's most prized collections were evacuated to Sverdlovsk (Yekaterinburg) in the Urals accompanied by their curators. The museum employees who remained in the Hermitage courageously attempted to safeguard the exhibits remaining there from bombs, shelling and from the dampness of deserted halls and buildings. Dying from hunger in the besieged city, scholars from the Hermitage did not cease their research work.

The war ended, the collections were brought back from evacuation and the restored halls began to radiate beauty. Already more than fifty years have passed from that tragic time. The Hermitage lives the routine life of a large museum: it collects, safeguards and studies the relics of world art and organizes exhibitions.

Thousands of visitors from all corners of the globe visit the Hermitage every year. For them the journey to the realm of treasures of world culture begins at the Winter Palace.

The Main (Jordan) Staircase
Decor of the ceiling

However, Rastrelli did not succeed in completing the palace interior decoration. After him several generations of the most illustrious architects worked on the decoration of its interiors. Only several rooms preserve the magnificent Baroque character conceived by Rastrelli. Above all, the Main Staircase. Already from afar, from the entrance gallery, its first steps are visible leading to the statue *Allegory of the State (Sovereignty)* on the lower landing. When having walked up to it, suddenly you emerge from the semi-darkness of the vaults into a brightly illuminated vast space spanning the entire height of the build-

The allegorical statue of Sovereignity on the landing of the Main (Jordan) Staircase

The Main (Jordan) Staircase in the Winter Palace

ing. There, on a height of almost 22 metres, Olympic gods soar in a blue sky of the painted ceiling, light pours through the windows and glides along the white walls with its gilt ornamentation and the statues of gods and muses. The white marble staircase with its carved balustrade leads into the state halls. In the eighteenth century it was called the Ambassadorial Staircase, and in the nineteenth century, the Jordan Staircase: during the winter, at the Epiphany, a holiday procession descended along it to the "Jordan font" cut through the ice on the Neva, where they bathed thus recalling the Baptism of Christ.

Edward Hau. 1807–1870
The Fieldmarshals Hall. 1866. Watercolour

The Large Coach.
France. 18th century

Two suites of main halls lead from the Main Staircase; one along the Neva, the other, the Great Suite of reception halls, leads into the depth of the palace. The Great Suite was created from the mid-eighteenth century to the close of the 1830s by the best architects of Russian Classicism. Vasily Stasov, who restored the halls after the fire of December 1837, deserves especially great commendation. He restored the appearance which had been conceived by his predecessors, bringing slight alterations to it corresponding to contemporary tastes. The suite of halls opens onto the Fieldmarshals Hall. Officers of the guard were on duty here, and the mounting of the palace guard also took place here. At that time portraits of Russian fieldmarshals hung on the walls.

The theme of martial glory, might and the majesty of the Russian Empire was central in the design of the palace official halls. It also is realized in the decoration of the neighbouring Memorial Room of Peter the Great. It is dedicated to the memory of Peter the Great, the first emperor of Russia. Peter is presented accompanied by Minerva in Jacopo Amigoni's painting in the niche of the hall; the emperor's throne is beneath the painting. Everywhere —in frescoes, in velvet wall panels embroidered in silver—the emblem of Peter I, the state emblems of the Russian Empire and laurel wreathes are present. The decor of the Armorial Hall embodies the unity of the empire. The chandeliers of this vast hall covering an area of 1,000 metres are ornamented with shields with the coat-of-arms of Russian gubernias. Here the emperor met his subjects, received the deputies of Russia's cities and the representatives of all the estates — the nobility, merchants and city dwellers. Next to the Armorial Hall is the Gallery of the Patriotic War of 1812, dedicated to Russia's victory over Napoleon's armies.

George Dawe
1781–1829
England
Portrait
of Mikhail
Barklay-de-Tolli
1829

*The 1812 Gallery
in the Winter Palace*

George Dawe
1781–1829
England
Portrait
of Mikhail Kutuzov
1829

332 portraits of Russian generals who participated in this war hang on its walls. The official portrait of Emperor Alexander I, under a canopy, hangs separately. A portrait of the Commander-in-Chief of the Russian Army, Mikhail Kutuzov, hangs in an honoured place before the entrance to the Great Throne Hall.

Konstantin Ukhtomsky. 1818–1881
The Big Throne (St.George) Hall in the Winter Palace
1862. Watercolour

The throne. Reconstruction. 1995

The Great Throne Hall, or the St. George Hall, is the most majestic and solemn hall of the palace. It is decorated with snow-white Carrara marble, set off with gilded bronze bases and capitals of the columns, cornices and the balusters of the balconies. The plated bronze ornamentation of the ceiling is mirrored in the parquet patterns, composed of sixteen different kinds of valuable woods. St. George slaying the Dragon—an ancient Russian state emblem personifying the might of Russia—is depicted over the site where the emperor's throne used to stand. The most important state acts and great receptions took place there.

Laurits Regner Tuxen. 1853–1927
Denmark
Wedding of Emperor Nicholas II and
Alexandra Fiodorovna
1895

Alexei Tyranov. 1808–1859
Russia
The Interior of the Great Church
in the Winter Palace. 1829

They were preceded as a rule by a service in the adjoining Great Church of the Winter Palace, which has preserved its Baroque decoration. In our day eighteenth-century Western European china is housed here. The main halls are used for displaying the exhibits: for example, the lavishly gilded and painted Great Carriage, created in the early eighteenth century by commission of Peter I in Paris, is kept in the Fieldmarshals Hall. It was used for Catherine II's outings during her coronation in Moscow in 1763. Similar carriages and coaches of the palace Carriage Coach-yard now comprise one of the most interesting collections in the Hermitage.

The sepulchre of Holy Prince Alexander Nevsky
Russia. 1747–56

The suite of state rooms along the Neva consists of three halls. The small Antechamber is decorated with a malachite rotunda, the work of nineteenth-century stone-cutters from the Urals. It was transferred here from the Cathedral of Our Lady of Kazan after the 1917 revolution. From the Antechamber the entrance leads to the Great, or St. Nicholas Hall, and then to the Concert Hall. The St. Nicholas Hall is the largest hall in the palace with an area of over 1,103 square metres. Court balls were held there, where up to 3,000 guests gathered. The silver sepulchre of Alexander Nevsky, the Russian thirteenth-century prince and military leader, is kept in the Concert Hall. It was transferred to the Hermitage from the Alexander Nevsky Monastery. At one time the guests invited to a ball or a reception waited there for the ceremonial exit of the imperial family from the inner, private chambers.

Icon of Holy Prince Alexander Nevsky
and St. Nicolas the Miracle-Worker
Russia. Late 19th century

Edward Hau. 1807–1870
England
The Rotunda in the Winter Palace
Watercolour

The round passage hall, the Rotunda, unites the Great Imperial part of the palace with the remaining living palatial quarters. The private entrance of Her Imperial Majesty leads to the state White Hall and Gold Drawing-Room of Empress Maria Alexandrovna, consort of Alexander II. Adjoining it, are the Green Dining-Room and the Study, upholstered with crimson damask, which frequently served for musical evenings. Further are the private chambers, the Boudoir and the Blue Bedroom.

The great imperial private chambers acquired their shape towards the outset of the nineteenth century. Alexander I and his spouse were the first to live there. After the 1837 fire the architect Alexander Briullov, who was entrusted with the restoration of the palatial living rooms, decorated these chambers for Empress Alexandra Fiodorovna, the consort of Nicholas I, anew. The splendid decor of the Malachite Drawing-Room has been preserved to our day. This room with its windows looking onto the Neva seems dazzlingly elegant thanks to the green malachite from the Urals which revetted the columns, fireplaces and tables. It harmonizes marvellously with the white walls, gilding, with the crimson upholstery of the furniture and draperies and with the patterned parquet. The last Russian emperor, Nicholas II, ordered the greater part of the rooms of the private imperial quarters to be redesigned in his taste—simply, and comfortably. In our day the Library of Nicholas II has been preserved, as well as the Private Dining-Room of the Emperor's family decorated in the eighteenth-century French Rococo style.

The Provisional Government under Alexander Kerensky was quartered in these rooms after the fall of the monarchy in 1917. Members of the government were arrested in the Private Dining-Room on October 26, 1917, during the night of the October coup d'état.

The Malachite Drawing-Room in the Winter Palace

*Paper weigt of malachite decorated
with a figure of a dancing girl
in Russian national dress
Russia. 1830s*

Vase
Russia. 19th century

The fireplace
in the Malachite Drawing-Room of the Winter Palace

36

The Gothic Library (Nicholas II's library) in the Winter Palace

The Gonzaga cameo
Alexandria
3rd century B.C.

The Gold Drawing-Room in the Winter Palace

41

The Pavilion Hall in the Small Hermitage

The idea of the creation of a "Hermitage" belonged to the first proprietress of the Winter Palace, Catherine II. This French word—*hermite*—means "the abode of a recluse", or "a place of solitude". In the eighteenth century it was used to designate secluded studies or park pavilions, where a selected social set gathered surrounded by pictures and rare objets d'art. Catherine decreed that a small building next to the Winter Palace should be built, which later was called the Small Hermitage. The Empress' first collections were kept in its Northern Pavilion, erected in 1767–69 by Jean-Baptiste Vallin de la Mothe. Her guests attended "small" Hermitage receptions in the small study. In accordance with etiquette for guests, composed by the hostess herself, the former were prescribed "to leave behind the doors, uniformly, all ranks, as well as hats and, in particular, rapiers", "to be gay", "to eat with relish and to drink to measure..." One large Pavilion Hall, created in the 1850s, is to be found here today. Bright and elegant, it is decorated with passage galleries, arcades and sparkling crystal chandeliers. The fountains near the walls let fall drops of water, recalling the Fountain of Tears of the Crimean khan's palace at Bakhchiserai. The floor is covered with copies of a mosaic floor of an ancient Roman bath. The Peacock Clock of an English eighteenth-century make, with moving figures of birds, which had been acquired by Catherine II, is displayed there now. The windows look out onto the Hanging Garden of the "Russian Semiramis". It was laid out on the volutes of the lower floor in 1764–69.

The Pavilion Hall in the Small Hermitage

"The Fountain of Tears" in the Pavilion Hall

The mosaic floor in the Pavilion Hall

Robert Campin. C. 1380–1444
The Netherlands
The St. Trinity
(left wing of a diptych). 1433–35

Robert Campin. C. 1380–1444
The Netherlands
The Virgin and Child by the Fireside
(right wing of a diptych). 1433–35

The Romanov Gallery
in the Small Hermitage

Flanking it, between the Northern and Southern pavilions, galleries were built for Catherine's growing collection in 1768–75. Even today they serve for displaying exhibitions. Now the exposition of Medieval Western European applied arts (5th–15th centuries)—church vessels, reliquaries, bronze water-carriers, enamels, china, stained-glass panels and tap-estries—is on display here. The exhibition of the fifteenth- and sixteenth-centuries Netherland art, small but providing a sufficiently full representation of the leading artists of Old Netherland painting, such as for example, Robert Campin, Rogier Van der Weyden, Hugo van der Goes and Lucas van Leyden, is also displayed there.

Reliquary with scenes
from the legend of St.Valeria
France
C. 1170

Rogier van der Weyden
1400–1464
The Netherlands
St. Luke Painting a Portrait of the Virgin

Simone Martini
C. 1284–1344
Italy
The Madonna *from* The Annunciation

In 1771–87 Yuri Velten built the Great (Old) Hermitage next to the Small Hermitage. The passage leads straight from the Pavilion Hall of the Small Hermitage to the Main Staircase of the Old Hermitage. It had been already built in the mid-nineteenth century when the State Council was located on the ground floor and to this day its name Sovetskaya (Council) has been preserved.

The staircase enclosed with open-worked cast-iron railings connects the vestibule with the upper landing decorated with sculptures, mosaic tables and a large vase of Ural malachite, a Russian nineteenth-century work. The entrance to the halls of the first floor is located here. In the eighteenth century they were a continuation of Catherine II's Hermitage. She organized "large" Hermitage receptions here, where up to 200 guests gathered. Her collections were also housed here. In the 1850s they were transferred to the New Hermitage, which had just been erected, and the abandoned rooms were once again redecorated by Andrei Stakenschneider for the heir to the throne. In our day the exhibition of the Italian Renaissance art (13th–16th centuries) is housed here. It begins with the Hall of the Primitives, i.e. the Protorenaissance art (13th–14th centuries), where the *Madonna* by Simone Martini belonging to the fourteenth-century Siennese School occupies a special place. This is the right fold of the diptych from the *Annunciation*; its left fold is in the National Gallery in Washington.

Fra Beato Angelico da Fiesole
1400–1455
Italy
Madonna and Child with St.Dominic
and St.Thomas Aquinas
1424–1430s
Fresco

Fra Philippo Lippi. 1406–1469
Italy
The Vision to St. Augustin

Bernardino Fungai
1460–1516
Italy
The Magnanimity of Scipio

The Hall of Italian Painting of the 16th Century in the Old Hermitage

The most famous part of the collection comprises the works of the great sixteenth-century Italian masters. The museum's jewel are the two pictures by Leonardo da Vinci (1452–1519) (out of not more than fourteen works remaining in the world). *The Madonna Benois*, purchased from the Benois family in St. Petersburg in 1914, was executed by the young Leonardo in 1478 in Florence. Through it he realized his knowledge of nature and man. His young Madonna playing with Her earnest and inquisitive son, incarnates the earthly beauty, youth and maternal joy. Acquired in 1865 in Italy from Count Litta, *The Madonna Litta*, in contrast, is the mature work of the artist, created in 1490 in Milan. The harmonic ideal of beauty of the Renaissance epoch is realized in the image of the inspired, beautiful woman, with a child in her arms. Both paintings are exhibited separately in a state hall. The columns of dark-grey granite on pedestals of red porphyry, white marble fireplaces with columns of red-green jasper effectively decorate the hall, while the ebony and mahogany impress one with the ornamentation made of tortoise-shell plates, copper and gilded bronze. The adjoining gallery houses paintings of the Venetian Renaissance School. Here one can admire Giorgione's enigmatic and magnificent *Judith* and nine pictures of the great Titian. Among them *Danaë*, *The Penitent Magdalene*, celebrating the charm and lofty fervency of feminine sentiments, and *St. Sebastian*, the well-known late artist's work.

Titian. 1485/90–1576
Italy
The Penitent Magdalene
1560s

Titian. 1485/90–1576
Italy
Danaë
Between 1546 and 1553

Giorgione
1478(?)–1510
Italy
Judith. C. 1504

Dish. Italy. 18th century

*The Raphael Loggias
in the New Hermitage*

The Raphael Loggias evoke still yet another genius of the Renaissance—a copy of the Vatican palace loggias painted by Raphael and his pupils in the early sixteenth century. In 1780–87 Raphael's frescoes were copied on canvas by order of Catherine II, brought to St. Petersburg and mounted on the volutes and walls of the gallery, specially built by Giacomo Quarenghi to the south of the Old Hermitage. Illuminated with light from the high windows, reflected in the mirrors, the gallery, with its semicircular arches, measuredly following one another, charms one with the pure and joyful colours of whimsical arabesque patterns. Paintings on Biblical themes, the renowned *Bible of Raphael*, are included in its decor. The neighbouring hall contains two pictures painted by Raphael himself.

*Raphael. 1483–1520
Italy
ıne Conestabile Madonna (Madonna with a Book)
C. 1503*

The Conestabile Madonna is especially famous, and was acquired by Emperor Alexander II for his spouse, Empress Maria Alexandrovna, in 1870 from the Conestabile family in Perugia. This small tondo is set into a gilded frame created after Raphael's drawing. Standing against the background of a springtime landscape, a slightly sorrowful Madonna, with an infant in her arms, seems an incarnation of purity and tenderness. The collection of Italian ceramics—more than 500 magnificent examples of Faenza, Urbino, Deruta and Castel-Durante ceramics—is also on exhibit here.

The Hall of Frescoes from the Raphael School in the New Hermitage

Michelangelo. 1475–1564
Italy
Crouching Boy
1530s

On the walls of the adjoining hall are copies of Raphael's Vatican frescoes created by his pupils. The *Crouching Boy* by the great Michelangelo, intended for the unfinished decoration of the Medici tomb in Florence, stands in the centre of the hall.

Main Staircase in the New Hermitage

Heinrich Imhoff. 1798–1869
Germany
Moses' Mother

The Raphael Loggias, the halls with his pictures and frescoes of his school, comprise a part of the New Hermitage. It was built in 1842–51 as a proper museum building by Vasily Stasov and Nikolai Yefimov after a project by Leo von Klenze, who designed the Munich Pinakothek. On February 5, 1852, the Imperial Public Museum was solemnly opened in the New Hermitage. In the early years of its existence visits to the museum were strictly regulated by the Office of the Court Ministry. Visitors were admitted only in uniforms, tail-coats and court attire. But as early as the 1860s entrance to the museum became free. The museum worked daily apart from holidays and those hours when "His Imperial Majesty deigned to visit the Hermitage".

The entrance to the museum was from quiet Millionnaya Street through the portico with the figures of ten granite atlantes. The vestibule of the Main Staircase, solemn and austere like the entrance to a temple, was behind it. Its walls were revetted with stucco imitating yellow marble, and twenty monolithic columns of grey granite towered above.

Burial urn in the shape of a reclining youth
Etruria. 4th century B.C.

The Twenty-Columned Hall in the New Hermitage

Red-figured pelike with a swallow
By Euphronius, Attica. 4th century B.C.

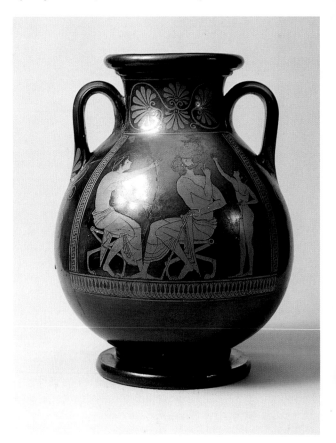

The halls on the ground floor, built for the keeping of ancient relics, now house the exhibitions of the Department of the Ancient World. The Twenty-Columned Hall, divided, like an ancient Greek temple, into three naves with granite columns, meant for collections of antique vases. The slender black-lacquered hydria from the 4th century B.C. from the town of Cumae, displayed here, was called the Queen of the Vases ("Regina vasorum"). On her dainty shoulders and grooved body there are delicately modelled reliefs, depicting Hellenic mysteries and a procession of wild beasts. This is one of the masterpieces in the collection of antique ceramics, which includes around 15,000 Ancient Greek, Etruscan and Italic vases.

Antique forms are imitated by Russian stone-carvers in their huge jasper vase weighing 19 tons, made in the Kolyvan Factory in the Altai mountains in 1831–43. The Kolyvan Vase adorns one of the halls of classical Roman art.

A rich collection of Ancient Roman marble sculpture is displayed in the halls, designed in the traditions of classical architecture. Conceived as a peristyle hall with sculpture, it recreates an inner courtyard of a Roman house. The collection of Roman sculptural portraits is especially famed; it includes about 120 pieces. A brilliant, slightly tired of life, young patrician, emperor Lucius Verus; an unknown, refined woman, nicknamed the "Syrian Woman", who is submerged in the world of complex moods; and many other pieces are presented in works of this collection.

Twenty centuries of the history of Ancient glyptics is reflected in the exhibition of gems, one of the best collections in the world. Its jewel, the Gonzaga Cameo (3rd century B.C.)—a double portrait of the Alexandrian Emperor Ptolemeus and his consort, Arsinoë, carved of a three-layered sardonyx. Being kept in the palace of Duke of Mantua, the cameo later turned up in the collection of Josephine Beauharnais, who then presented it to Russian Emperor Alexander I.

A separate part of the exhibition is dedicated to the culture of the cities of the Northern Black Sea coast, founded by the Greeks in the 7th–6th centuries B.C. Russian archaeologists brought remarkable relics of ancient sculpture and handicrafts from there. In the burial tomb of a Greek noblewoman from the fifth century B.C. a rare painted vessel in the form of a sphinx with the head of a girl was found among grave goods. Archaeological excavations became a source of a unique collection of ancient Greek jewellery. In the burial-mound of Kul-Oba near Kerch gold pendants from the 5th century B.C. were discovered. The head of the famous statue of Athena of Parthenos by the great Athenian sculptor Pheidias was reproduced on the medallion.

The Jupiter Hall in the New Hermitage

74

Philippe the Arabe
Rome. 3rd century

Portrait of a man. Rome
1st century B.C.

Terracotta statuette. Tanagra
4th–3rd centuries B.C.

Heracles slaying the Lion.
Roman copy of the 4th century B.C.
after the original by Lysippus

*Gold clasp in the shape
of a curling panther
from the Siberian Collection of Peter I
4th–3rd centuries B.C.*

*Gold belt-plate
with a scene of hunting in a wood
from the Siberian Collection of Peter I
4th–3rd centuries B.C.*

*Gold vessel
decorated with depictions of Scythian warriors
4th century B.C.*

*Gold comb
from the Scythian burial-mound of Solokha
4th century B.C.*

*The silver amphore
from the Scythian burial-mound of Chertomlyk
4th century B.C.*

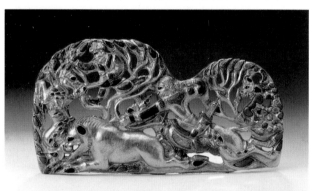

**Gallery
of the History of Ancient Painting
in the New Hermitage**

**Antonio Canova. 1757–1822
Italy
Cupid and Psyche**

**Berthel Thorwaldsen. 1768/70–1844
Denmark
A Shepherd**

The first floor of the New Hermitage was specially designed for a picture gallery. The entrance to it is from the Main Staircase through the Gallery of the History of Ancient Painting exhibiting the pictures on its walls recreating Ancient Greek painting. They were created after the descriptions in Ancient texts in the encaustic technique, i.e. with wax paints upon warmed up copper boards. The gallery, painted with antique patterns, is adorned with malachite vases. The exhibition of the 18th- to the early 19th-century West European sculpture is to be found there. The works of the Italian sculptor Antonio Canova are especially alluring. One of his masterpieces is the marble group *Three Graces*—the three beautiful companions of Venus: Beauty, Joy and Charm.

The Large Skylights in the New Hermitage

Carravaggio. 1571–1610
Italy
The Lute Player. C. 1595

From reminiscences about ancient painting, the visitor goes on to Western European painting when entering the central halls of the Picture Gallery—the Skylights. These comprise three large halls, illuminated by natural light through glass ceilings. They were decorated with palatial splendour because at some time the museum was considered to be "a continuation of the Tsarist residence". The vases and tables made of Badakhshan lazarite and green malachite from the Urals, standard lamps of dark pink rhodonite and the grey-green Korgon porphyry in the Small and Large Skylights imbue a especial glitter to the decoration. The pictures by Italian artists of the late 16th to the 18th centuries are exhibited there; they are a continuation of the exhibition of Italian art in the Old Hermitage. Here one can see Carravaggio's *The Lute Player* where the lyrical mood of the musician is brilliantly revealed.

*Giovanni Battista
Tiepolo
1696–1770
Italy
Triumph of the
Emperor
C. 1725*

El Greco (Domenikos Theotokopoulos)
1541–1614
Spain
The Apostles Peter and Paul
Between 1587 and 1592

Diego Velázquez. 1599–1660
Spain
Breakfast. 1617/18

Bartolomé Esteban Murillo. 1617–1682
Spain
Boy with a Dog. 1650s

The third skylight houses the Spanish 15th- to early 19th-century masterpieces. The Apostle Peter radiating the warmth of Christian love and the passionate preacher Paul are presented in El Greco's painting. The limitless expanses of Spain unfold behind the back of St. Lawrence, ready to endure martyrdom in the monumental canvas by Francisco de Zurbarán. There are two pictures belonging to the brush of Diego Velázquez—*Portrait of Count Olivares* and his youthful work, *Breakfast*, a vitally spontaneous, as well as symbolic, scene.

Peter Paul Rubens. 1577–1640
Flanders
Portrait of a Lady-in-Waiting to the Infanta Isabella
Mid-1620s

Five halls of the New Hermitage are taken over by the exhibits of 17th-century Flemish art. More than 500 pictures by almost 140 artists constitute this unique collection, one of the finest in the world.

A separate hall is dedicated to Peter Paul Rubens, the head and founder of a school. 42 of his paintings, from early to the final works, give a full and many-sided presentation of the "king of painters".

Peter Paul Rubens. 1577–1640
Flanders
The Union of Earth and Water. C. 1618

One of his best pictures is *Perseus and Andromeda*, created in the 1620s. Rubens was then at the zenith of his glory, in love, felicitous: he had only just wedded to the delightful Elena Fourmen, the model of his captivating female images. The colour resounds triumphantly in the full mighty movement of the composition, glorifying the hero's valour, who received Andromeda's tender love as a recompense.

Portrait of a Lady-in-Waiting to the Infanta Isabella charms one by the profusion of inner feelings on the young woman's visage. This is the traditional title of this famous portrait which might possibly be a por-trayal of Rubens' daughter, who died early. It was executed on the basis of a drawing created in her life-time and from the imagination of the artist and father. One of Rubens' celebrated masterpieces, *Bacchus*, was painted at the end of his life. The Ancient god surrounded by his companions is the personification of the material, carnal origins of nature, almost burdening his corpulent body. The artist's sketches preserve the spontaneity of conception of the great painter, including those for the pictures belonging to the cycle *Life of Maria Medici* in the Louvre, Paris.

The Van Dyck Room in the New Hermitage

Twenty-four pictures by Anthonis van Dyck, the most independent pupil of Rubens, a famous European portraitist, cover the walls of an entire hall. Both chamber and magnificent official portraits painted at the English King's Court (*Portrait of Count Thomas Whorton*) are found here.

The Snyders Room in the New Hermitage

Jacob Jordaens. 1593–1678
Flanders
The Bean King. C. 1638

In the collection of paintings by Jacob Jordaens (1593–1678), who became the "leading painter of Antwerp" after Rubens, the widely famous *Bean King*, the colourful, rich depiction of a national Flemish celebration, takes pride of place. Still-lifes by Frans Snyders, *Hunting Scene* by of Paul de Voos, and works by Teniers and Brouwer hang next to the paintings by Jordaens. The Dutch 17th- and 18th-century school of painting is presented in no less comprehensive a fashion. It includes more than one thou-sand pictures. The Tent Hall in the New Hermitage was built especially for the pictures of the Minor Dutch school. All genres of paintings are represent-ed in this collection. The art of portraiture is pre-sented by two chef-d'oeuvres by Frans Hals (*Portrait of a Man* and *Portrait of a Young Man Holding a Glove*) and by other portraitists. Among numerous land-scapes the works of Jacob van Ruisdael stand out. His best work *The Marsh* is a profound philosophical reflection by the artist on nature, life and death.

Frans Hals. 1581/85–1666
Holland
Portrait of a Young Man Holding a Glove
C. 1650

Frans Snyders. 1579–1657
Flanders
Fruit in a Bowl on a Red Table-cloth

The Tent-Room in the New Hermitage

The "quiet life" of the Dutch still-life is reflected in a multitude of works, one of the masterpieces among them is Willem Heda's *Breakfast with a Lobster* where the objects, bathing in soft silver light, have been placed with a deliberate carelessness on a table Favourite Dutch genre scenes by Jan Steen, Pieter de Hooch (*A Woman and Her Maid*), Gerard Terborch, Adriaen van Ostade are also found here.

Pieter de Hooch. 1629–1684
Holland
A Woman and Her Maid. C. 1660

Jan van Huysum. 1659–1716
Holland
Flowers

Pieter Claesz. 1597–1661
Holland
Breakfast with Ham. 1647

Aert van der Neer
1603/04–1677
Holland
A Moonlit Night

Jacob Isaaksz van Ruisdael
1628/29–1682
Holland
River in a Forest. 1670s

Rembrandt Harmensz van Rijn. 1606–1669
Holland
The Holy Family. 1645

Rembrandt Harmensz van Rijn. 1606–1669
Holland
David's Farewell to Jonathan. 1642

Rembrandt Harmensz van Rijn. 1606–1669
Holland
The Return of the Prodigal Son. 1668–69

Twenty-four paintings by Rembrandt, one of the best collections in the world, occupy a separate hall. The entire creative path of the great Dutch painter passes before one's eyes with an entire constellation of masterpieces. His early picture *Flora* was painted in the year of the artist's wedding to Saskia van Uylenborch. He depicted his young wife in the sumptuous attire of a goddess with a slightly timid, feminine expression upon a softly illuminated visage. The pride of the collection, created in his mature years, is *Portrait of an Old Man in Red*. Immersed in thought, on the border between light and darkness, life and death, the old man, bearing the yoke of life, is one of the most penetrating and profound images in Rembrandt's art. The protagonist of Rembrandt's most famous painting, *The Return of the Prodigal Son* possesses affinity to it. Painted at the close of the artist's difficult life, rejected in its time, this monumental depiction of an Evangelical scene became the expression of his deep faith in the beauty of human kindness and love.

Rembrandt Harmensz van Rijn. 1606–1669
Holland
Flora. 1634

Rembrandt Harmensz van Rijn. 1606–1669
Holland
Portrait of an Old Jew. 1654

Antoine Watteau. 1684–1721
France
A Capricious Woman. C. 1718

The New Hermitage was unable to accommodate the growing collection after 1917. In 1922 the Winter Palace was handed over to the Hermitage by a governmental decree. The exhibition of the French 15th- to 18th-century art, the second most important in the world after the Louvre collection, was displayed in the reserve living quarters with their windows overlooking Palace Square, where Empress Catherine II had resided in the 18th century and which was redecorated in 1837. The works of almost all the French artists are presented here. Twelve pictures acquaint one with the art of Nicolas Poussin, the founder of the French painting school. In one of his best pictures, *Tancred and Erminia*, he ardently and convincingly affirms the beauty of self-sacrifice. Almost all of Antoine Watteau's (1684–1721) eight paintings, which can be considered his masterpieces, are kept here. Watteau was one of a poetic painters of France. Such is his *A Capricious Woman*—a graceful and ironic *scène galante*.

Nicolas Poussin. 1594–1665
France
Tancred and Erminia. 1630s

110

Nicolas Lancret. 1690–1743
France
La Camargo

Nicolas Poussin. 1594–1665
France
Landscape with Polyphemus. 1649

Louis Le Nain. 1593–1648
France
A Milkwoman's Family. 1640s

Claude Gellée, called Lorrain. 1600–1682
France
Morning in a Harbour. 1640s

Etiénne Maurice Falconet. 1716–1791
France
Cupid Wagging His Finger. 1758

Exhibition of French Art
of the 17th–18th Centuries

Two genre scenes (*The Laundress* and *Grace Before Meal*) and the still-life commissioned by Catherine II represent the serious, pure, humane art of Jean-Baptiste Siméon Chardin. The works of painters hang side by side with outstanding works by leading French sculptors. The jewel of the exhibition is a statue of Voltaire by Jean Antoine Houdon. It is a duplicate of a statue in the foyer of the Comédie-Française in Paris, executed by Houdon on commission of Catherine II.

Marie Louise-Elisabeth Vigée-Lebrun. 1755–1842
France
Portrait of Grand Duchesses Alexandra Pavlovna
and Yelena Pavlovna, Daughters of Paul I. 1796

Jean Honoré Fragonard. 1732–1806
France
A Stolen Kiss

Jean Antoine Houdon. 1741–1828
France
Voltaire

Mantel clock **Cupid and Psyche. *1799***
Workshop of Pierre Philip Thomir, France

The collection of the applied arts of France is rich
and varied: Limoges enamels and Saint-Porchère
faience, the largest in the world collection of 17th-
and 18th-century silver, furniture, tapestries, fabrics,
embroideries, lace and jewellery. A separate suite
of halls was assigned for this collection. The magnificent collection of French graphics, kept in the
Departments of Drawing and Engravings, comple-
ments this exhibition which in particular comprises
one of the best collections of French 16th-century
pencil portraiture: the works of François Clouet
(*Portrait of Charles IX*) and other masters.

Exhibition of French Art of the 17th–18th Centuries

Ambrosius Golbein. C.1495–C.1519
Germany
Portrait of a Young Man

Caspar David Friedrich
1774–1840
Germany
On the Sailing Vessel

The Exhibition
of German Art
of the 16th Century

The exhibition of German 15th- to 18th-century and English 15th- to 19th-century art adjoins the French ones. The works of German Renaissance masters are of special interest, in particular five works by Lucus Cranach the Elder. Painted in 1509, *Venus and Cupid*, is the first depiction of a naked goddess in German art. In accordance with the widespread interpretation of Venus' image in Germany, Cranach imbues his slender goddess with a somewhat menacing countenance. The inscription above her head warns: "Drive away all the temptations of Cupid so that Venus will not take possession of your dazzled heart."

The exhibits of English art occupies four halls. The pearl of the collection is *Portrait of a Lady in Blue* by Thomas Gainsborough painted masterfully in cold silver-blue tones. Side by side with painting and sculpture, china and faience, one of the best collections of English silver is housed here. A huge silver wine-cooler weighing more than two hundred kilos, standing on figures of lions and decorated with Bacchanal scenes, is executed by Charles Kendler in the first half of the 18th century.

The exhibition of Contemporary Art of the 19th–20th centuries is located on the second floor. The largest collection of French Impressionism, Post-Impressionism and early 20th-century masters is housed here. These paintings were collected at the border of the 19th and 20th centuries by Moscow collectors, Sergei Shchukin and the Morozov brothers, Ivan and Mikhail. Nationalized after the 1917 revolution, they constituted the Museum of Contemporary Western Art in Moscow. After its closure in 1948 the collections were divided between the State Museum of Fine Art in Moscow and the Hermitage. The heroic struggle of French painters for a new, contemporary art, is reflected in the Hermitage in works by leading artists. Eight pictures by Claude Monet reveal the formation of the Impressionist method. The companion pictures, *Corner of the Garden at Montgerons* and *Pond in Mongerons*, created in 1876, marked the blossoming of Impressionism: from scattered fine coloured dabs, hurled onto the canvas, a lively and palpitating world of nature is born, infused with sunlight and fanned by the wind. The most renowned of six pictures by Auguste Renoir is *Portrait of the Actress Jeanne Samary*. The play of light and colour is evoked by a charming femininity and the elusive delicate mood of the young actress, depicted in the foyer of the theatre.

Eleven pictures by Cézanne—landscapes, portraits and still-lifes—reveal the talent of the great Post-Impressionist master to the fullest. His *Great Pine-Tree in Aix*, represents a tree warmed by the sun, inserting its hand-like branches in the goldish distances and blue sky of Provence, and is an embodiment of living energy and strength. Dutch by nationality, Van Gogh became a great French artist. *Ladies of Arles,* created, as his other three pictures, at the zenith of his talent, in Provence in 1888, hang next to the peasant woman of his Dutch drawings. A single violently flourishing earth cultivated by human hands united them. All twenty-five of Paul Gauguin's pictures were painted in Oceania, where he set off, realizing his dream about "a piece of earth untouched by civilization". His *Tahitian Pastorales* is an embodiment in colour of an acquired faith of the artist in the harmony of the universe.

The sculptures of Auguste Rodin are assigned an entire hall. Like his contemporary Impressionists he strove to imbue life with movement (*Eternal Spring*), subordinating it to marble and bronze.

The extensive division of the exhibition acquaints one with the early art of the best 20th-century masters. The famous French painter Henri Matisse once said: "My best works are in the Leningrad". One of his thirty-seven works is *Red Room*. Its protagonist, red colour, subordinates all the hues to itself. Colour harmony here is not the virtue of a beautiful interior but the sign of beauty, not formal but infused with the warmth of human existence. Some thirty works by Pablo Picasso represents the Red, Blue and Cubist periods of his art. *Lady with a Fan* is one of the most famous works of Cubism. The picture contains an allusion to the theme (its second title is *After the Ball*), but it does not contain a narrative: the objective construction of the female image is naked. The great sound of a mighty symphony in the *Composition No. 6* by the founder of Abstractionism, Vasily Kandinsky, completes the exhibition of art from the nineteenth—early twentieth centuries. Adjoining it is the hall dedicated to contemporary Italian art. Geometrically strict forms and the pure colour of the *Metaphysical Still-Life* by Georges Morandi reveals the talent of one of the founders of the "metaphysical painting". A vast section comprises the works of outstanding 20th-century sculptors.

The Arabic Hall in the Winter Palace

The exhibits from the Department of the History of Russian Culture of the 6th–early 20th centuries is located on the first floor of the palace—relics of the applied arts and mode of life, technology and sciences, paintings and sculptural portraits, drawings and engravings. The Sections of Slavonic and Old Russian Culture are side by side with the objects of crafts, ancient Rusian frescoes and around one thousand icons, which includes a not inconsiderable number of veritable masterpieces. Numerous exhibits tell about Peter I's era (the first quarter of the 18th century) including personal and memorial items belonging to Peter himself. One of the halls is designed like an interior of a wealthy house of that period. A table with folded painted leafs, executed for Peter by craftsmen from Arkhangelsk, is in the centre; and one of the first Russian tapestries depicting Peter I at the Battle of Poltava hangs on the wall. A bronze bust of Peter I is an outstanding work of the Italian sculptor Bartholomeo Carlo Rastrelli (the father of the architect), invited to Russia by Peter and working here all his life.

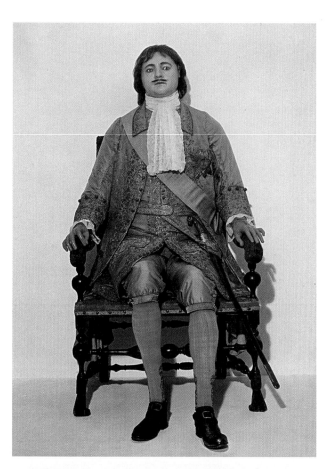

Bartholomeo Carlo Rastrelli
1675–1744
"Wax person of Peter I". 1732

Jean Marc Nattier. 1685–1766
France
Portrait of Catherine I. 1717

Among pieces of furniture, costumes, china, silver, carved bone, Tula steel and others, which present the "century of Empresses" (the reign of Elizabeth Petrovna and Catherine II) with pageantry, the portraits, often created by the best 18th-century painters, are of especial interest. One of them, Ivan Vishniakov's portrait of Stepanida Yakovleva, the fiance of the son of a Petersburg merchant, unites in itself the devices of the European portrait with elements of the ancient Russian *parsuna*. The private chambers of Nicholas I's family are occupied by the exhibition "Russian Nineteenth-Century Interiors", combining furniture, tapestries, china and portraiture. These are items from the Winter Palace and other Tsarist residences and private palaces and mansions of St. Petersburg.

Bouquet of precious stones. Russia. 1740

Ivan Vishniakov
1688–1761
Russia
Portrait of Stepanida Yakovleva. C. 1756

Cabinet. Russia. 1750–1770s

Fragment of a felt carpet
of the 5th–4th centuries B.C.
From the Pazyryk burial-mound

The ground floor of the Winter Palace is under the disposal of the Archaeological Department. Its exhibitions include objects of Primitive Culture from the Paleolithic era to the first centuries of our millennium, discovered by archaeologists (or accidentally) on the territory of Russia, Ukraine or the Black Sea Coast. One of the halls contains the finds from the burial-mound of a leader from the 5th–4th centuries B.C., unearthed between 1929 and 1954 in a barrow in the Pazyryk settlement in the Altai. The permafrost formed in the grave preserved unique objects of ancient art: a huge felt carpet of local workmanship, a wooden funeral chariot, ornaments in the Animal Style of wood, leather, felt, Chinese silk and also the oldest in the world wool pile Persian (or Middle Asian) carpet. The culture of the Scythian nomad tribes dwelling in the steppes of the Black Sea coast between the 7th and the 3rd centuries B.C. is presented in an extensive exhibition of objects from Scythian burial-mounds and settlements. The famous collection of Scythian gold is kept in a special storeroom. The gold pendant in the form of a deer from the late 7th century B.C. is a masterpiece of the Scythian Animal Style. It was discovered in 1897 near Kostromskaya settlement in the Northern Caucasus. The deer decorating the shield of a Scythian warrior was considered a solar symbol, signifiying the positive forces of nature. The outer appearance of the Scythians, their character are magnificently evoked in their depiction decorating the gold comb of the 4th-century B.C. from the Solokha barrow unearthed in 1912–13 on the bank of the Dnieper. This is a masterpiece from the Bosporus kingdom, established by the Greeks in the Crimea in the 6th century B.C.

The Oriental Department boasts more than 150,000 objects of art and culture of the peoples of the East. The art of the ancient Orient—Egypt and Mesopotamia—is exhibited on the ground floor of the Winter Palace. The relatively small collections reflect all the historical stages of Ancient Egyptian art. The collection of sculptures—statues, portraits, reliefs from palaces and tombs, bronze and clay statuettes—as well as painted sarcophagi, papyri and Fayum portraits, relating to the later period of the 1st–3rd centuries A.D., and Coptic cloths from Christian Egypt (4th–9th centuries) are of great interest.

The exhibition devoted to the art of Central Asian countries is on the ground floor also. Among the manifold exhibits—items of ceramic and metal, carpets, weapons and others—the enormous frescoes with depictions of hunting scenes and festivals, which once decorated in the 5th–7th centuries the walls of the palaces of dignitaries excavated in the ancient town of Pendjkent, occupy a special place.

The exhibition of Byzantine art (4th–15th centuries) occupies three halls on the second floor of the Winter Palace. It is a marvellous collection of silver ecclesiastical vessels, enamels, articles of carved bone and icons. The best icon in the collection, the icon of St. Gregory the Thaumaturgist (12th century), is dis-

tinguished by a delicateness of brushwork, wealth of colours and an especial intellectuality of the image. A large exhibition of art of Near Eastern countries is housed in the neighbouring halls. The exhibits of Iranian art contain one of the best collections in the world of silver articles from the Sassanid dynasty era (3rd–7th centuries). Among their masterpieces is a dish with a depiction of Emperor Shapur II (309–379) hunting.

The second floor also houses a rich exhibit from Far Eastern countries—China, Tibet, Mongolia, India, Indonesia and Japan. The Chinese articles embrace the period from the 13th century B.C. to the begin-ning of the 20th century, these are china, enamel, carved stones, and lacquerware adjoining paintings and items of plastic arts.

Unique objects were collected by Russian scholars during expeditions. Murals, painted loess statuettes and two clay figures of fantastic beasts—Guardians of Buddha's Throne—were delivered in 1914–15 from Turkestan from the Cave Monastery of the Thousand Buddhas in Dun Xuang (4th century). The collection of paintings includes both a marvellous collection of Buddhist icons and 11th- to 15th-century secular paintings on silk, as well as works of contemporary painters.

China. Unknown artist. 15th–18th centuries
*Portrait of an Official of the 5th Rank
and His Wife*

Dish
painted with peonies and bamboo
China. 18th century

Vases
of crystal and amethyst
China. 18th century

Vases
of chalcedone and nephrite
China. 18th century

Vase painted with a scene of polo game
Iran. 13th century

Ring
for the shooting from a bow
Iran. 13th century

Bronze kettle
Herat, Iran. 1163

Glass lamp
Egypt or Syria. 14th century

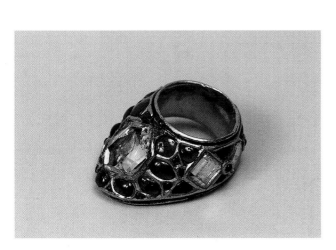

Ο ΑΓΙΟC ΓΡΗΓΟΡΙΟC Ο ΘΟΜΑΤΥΡΓΟC

136

Jamashita Rijn
1857–1939
Icon of The Resurrection of Christ
C. 1891

Icon of St.Gregory the Thaumaturgist
Byzantium
12th century

The Hermitage Theatre is an inseparable part of the Hermitage. It was built in 1783–87 by the architect Giacomo Quarenghi by the order of Catherine II. The theatre is connected with the Old Hermitage by the gallery on the arch over the Winter Canal where the theatre foyer is housed. Catherine II organized suppers in it after performances which generally consummated the Hermitage reception. In 1902 Leonty Benois designed the foyer in the style of French eighteenth-century Rococo. From the foyer one can enter the authentic 18th-century theatre hall. It was built in the form of an ancient amphitheatre: six rows of benches descend onto a small pit in front of the stage—armchairs were placed here for the Empress. In our day performances are staged in the theatre and public lectures are read. The hall and stage were built by Quarenghi in the Winter Palace of Peter I which was located at this site so that its socle part was preserved. Almost 200 years later, in 1987–89 during the restoration of the theatre the private chambers of Peter I, which had been located here, were reconstructed and opened for visitors. The "wax person" of the emperor was placed in his study—a depiction of Peter I in his natural size of wood and wax, executed in 1732 by Carlo Bartholomeo Rastrelli. The "person" is arrayed in the formal dress of Peter I with a ribbon and star of the order of St. Andrew the First-Called.

The Menshikov Palace

The spirit of the Petrine epoch is revived in the chambers of the Menshikov Palace, one of the first palaces of St. Petersburg, which was built in the 1710s–1720s for the first Petersburg Governor-General, the closest associate of Peter I, Alexander Menshikov. The recreated part of the private chambers, official and servant quarters, as a result of the restoration in the 1950–1970s, provides an idea about the life of their brilliant proprietor—one of the most striking personalities of the Petrine era.

From the formal antechamber decorated with antique sculptures, which alongside with other works of

art Menshikov collected following an example of his great patron, Peter I, the oak stairway leads to the first floor, where the Great Hall was located. Light, with gilt ornamentations and mirrors, the hall was used for receptions and "assemblies" at which Peter gathered all the nobilities of the new capital by his order. The living quarters of the owner were also on the first floor. In the suite of living rooms, the Walnut Study lavishly decorated with a panel of different kinds of precious wood, placed between the pilasters with carved gilded capitals, is especially alluring.

The State Hermitage is not only a world famous museum. It comprises a unique realm, a special page of Russian history. The founder of St. Petersburg, Peter I, died here, Catherine the Great directed affairs of state and Nicholas II inaugurated the first State Duma. These walls recall Alexander I, the victor over Napoleon, the Tsar-Liberator Alexander II, who died from wounds, and the arrest of the Provisional Government by revolutionary soldiers and sailors in 1917. These walls also recall the terrible days of the Great Patriotic War when museum workers, who were dying of hunger, salvaged monuments of art for posterity. In creating its interiors, the architects, sculptors, artists and decorators, who conceived

this magnificent ensemble, realized their ideas about the beautiful; they carried the spirit of an era long passed down to us and established that special inner world which underscores the value of works of art and allows one on every occasion to apprehend their significance. The curators and keepers of the Hermitage collections, as well as all other members of the stuff, do their best in keeping the traditions of their predecessors trying not only to preserve the great heritage of the past but to develop the museum according to new trends. At the same time nobody forgets that the Hermitage is not only a world-famous museum, but an evidence of Russian history which must be dear to every Russian.

Index of Paintings and Sculptures Reproduced